MarcoPolo

WRITTEN and ILLUSTRATED by

Demi

MARSHALL CAVENDISH CHILDREN

IN THE SAN SEVERO PARISH of Venice, Italy, Marco Polo was born in 1254 to a family of wealthy merchants. His father, Niccolo, and his uncle Maffeo, were traders who traveled to Constantinople, Persia, and China.

They were gone for so long that Marco did not meet his father and uncle until they returned to Venice in 1269. By then, Marco was fifteen years old.

Two years later, in 1271, Marco, his father, Niccolo, his uncle Maffeo, and several servants began their famous trip to China. The great emperor of China, Kublai Khan, was tolerant of all religions. He had asked Niccolo and Maffeo Polo to return to China with holy oil from the tomb of Jesus. He also wanted them to bring one hundred Christian men, so he could learn if the Christian faith was the true religion. If it was, Kublai Khan and all his people would become Christians. The Polos packed food, clothing, medicine, crystal, and jewels to trade. They also carried letters and gifts from Pope Gregory X for Emperor Kublai Khan.

The three Polos set sail for the Holy Land. In Jerusalem there was a cave in the Church of the Holy Sepulcher where Jesus had been buried. From a lamp that burned in that cave, the Polos collected the holy oil.

The Polos found only two Dominican monks willing to travel with them. They set sail for Acre on an armed galley ship under the protection of the king of Armenia, who regarded the Polos as ambassadors of the pope.

At Ayas they disembarked and traveled by horses and pack mules toward Armenia. But the monks became terrified of marauding Egyptian Muslim bandits known as Mamluks and demanded that they be sent home. The Polos found a group of Crusaders, the Knights Templars, to escort the terrified monks back to Jerusalem.

Narrowly escaping the Mamluk
bandits, the Polos traveled through
eastern Turkey and Armenia and saw
where Noah's ark had settled on top
of Mount Ararat after the great flood.

Niccolo and Maffeo Polo already knew the road ahead. They were brilliant explorers, knowing the ways and customs of people, and they were gifted at speaking many languages. Their safety was helped by the letters they carried from Pope Gregory X and the two protective gold tablets they carried from the Chinese emperor Kublai Khan.

Farther east, between the Black and Caspian seas, Marco saw fountains of oil springing from the ground, and for the first time he saw how people used oil for light and to cure skin diseases. Marco began writing down these wonders in his journal.

In Tabriz the Polos bartered in Persian and Arabic for precious pearls. In Baghdad they were dazzled by clothes made of gold and silk and a very fine cotton material called muslin, which was cool to wear in summer. In Kerman they traded turquoise stones for fine swords of steel.

Riding through high mountain passes, they shivered with cold before reaching the scorching hot Rudbar Plain. They traveled past date trees, oxen called zebus, and large sheep with thirty-pound tails.

On the Rudbar Plain their caravan was attacked in a dust storm by terrible bandits called Karunas. The Polos barely escaped, and most of the people in their caravan were murdered or sold into slavery.

Lucky to be alive, the Polos headed south to Hormuz on the Persian Gulf. There, it was so hot, people spent the day in water up to their chins. The Polos tried to hire a ship to carry them eastward to India, but they found only flimsy barges with hulls sewn together with coconut twine instead of joined with iron nails. And so they had to retrace their steps to Kerman in eastern Persia, where they traded some of their horses for camels to carry them by land along the ancient Silk Route. Used for centuries by traders carrying goods between the East and West, the Silk Route was filled with risk, danger, and adventure.

Now the Polos crossed a vast salt desert, the Desert of Emptiness, which had pools of poisonous green water. After many weeks of scorching dry heat, they came to Tunocain, which was lush and green. Marco thought the women there were the most beautiful in the world. Tunocain was home to a Muslim sect called the Assassins who terrorized their enemies. Their leader was known as the Old Man of the Mountains and was feared by all.

Continuing along the Silk Route, the Polos left Persia and entered what today is called Afghanistan. In the beautiful mountains of Badakshan, they found mines that yielded shining rubies and sapphires. Marco fell ill from exhaustion and bad food and water, and so the Polos rested for one year in the mountains. When Marco recovered, they continued their journey. They followed the Oxus River northeast and climbed higher and higher into the Pamir Mountains—"the rooftop of the world." At 20,000 feet, it was so high and so cold that no birds flew, fire did not burn, and it was impossible to cook food.

Coming down the eastern slopes, the Polos arrived at Kashgar on the edge of China. Following the Silk Route southeast, they passed Kotan, named for its abundant cotton, and saw people mining precious jades of yellow, green, and black. The Polos rested their camels and mules for a week at Lop Nor in preparation for crossing the treacherous great Gobi Desert, where everything would be terribly hot, flat, dry, and sandy.

The three Polos plodded along the vast stretches among the twenty-eight water holes of the Taklimakan Desert. Marco wrote of eerie spirit voices that tried to lead them astray. Whistling, singing sands confused their hearing, and mirages confused their sight. Finally, they reached Sha-cow and rested. There, Marco saw asbestos for the first time in his life. He was amazed that it did not burn. Mined from mountains, it was dried, pounded, and woven into cloth.

Also for the first time, Marco saw strange shaggy animals, or yaks, and musk antelope prized for their perfume. He saw Mongols living in great round tents called yurts. The Mongols were superb horsemen, hunters, and archers who chased their prey across the plains. They were also skilled organizers and fierce fighters. Marco could see why they were called "masters of the biggest half of the world."

In 1275 news reached the great Khan that the Polos were at the Chinese border. He sent a party to escort them to his summer palace in Shangtu, also known as Xanadu. After forty days of traveling in comfort, they arrived at Shangtu. Marble steps and golden halls led to the vast court chamber where Emperor Kublai Khan sat on a high throne surrounded by courtiers. The emperor was delighted to see Niccolo and Maffeo after so many years, and he greeted them warmly. The Polos presented the mighty Khan with the gifts from Pope Gregory X and set before him the sacred oil from Jerusalem.

Every year on August 28, Kublai Khan left Shangtu for the capital city of Khanbalik. Marco declared Kublai's palace the most beautiful he'd ever seen. Made with gorgeous gold and silver, marble and pearl, gems and jewels, it was heaven on earth. Emperor Kublai Khan had four wives by whom he had twenty-two sons that he treated equally. All the children showed the greatest respect for their parents and grandparents. The Khan held splendid banquets, with magicians, actors, jugglers, and acrobats. On New Year's Day the emperor paraded his five thousand elephants through Khanbalik, wishing everyone happiness and distributing gifts. He canceled the taxes owed by victims of bad weather and crop failures and instead gave them food and clothes from the imperial store-houses. "No one is denied," declared Marco Polo.

The Khan built hospitals, schools, and the Grand Canal from Khanbalik to Kinsai. Thousands of ships sailing on the canal greatly increased trade throughout his empire. Kublai Khan tolerated all religions: Taoism, Buddhism, Confucianism, Christian Nestorianism, Islam, Judaism, and all sects. He treated them equally. He also studied science and built a high observatory from which to study and chart the stars.

Marco was fascinated by Chinese inventions: gunpowder, the kite, the pony express, little black stones that burned all night (coal), spaghetti, the water clock, the umbrella, silk, the spinning wheel, paper, the compass, the printing press, and even a wheelbarrow with a sail!

Marco joined the emperor Kublai Khan on his hunting expeditions, where a cheetah always sat right behind the emperor ready to spring and kill its prey. Marco learned the Mongol language and the ways of the imperial court so quickly that the Khan decided to send young Marco as his ambassador to distant parts of the empire. Marco proved so bright and so quick and gave such vivid and true reports to the emperor that he gained the Khan's complete trust and would serve as his ambassador for the next seventeen years.

Crossing the Great Yellow River and the Yangtze—"the mightiest river in the world"—Marco traveled into the western provinces and as far off as Tibet. He recorded the customs and ways of everything he saw: tattooed men and devil dancers, lions with stripes (which in fact were tigers), panda bears, and bamboo. Marco saw "snakes and serpents of vast size," which were really pythons and crocodiles. He also saw "a very ugly unicorn that looked like a pig," which was a rhino. Going south to Burma, Marco was amazed by the huge numbers of gold and silver Buddhist temples and pagodas.

Marco returned to Kublai Khan's court four months later, and Marco's amazing report impressed the emperor so much that he gave Marco a noble title and an important place on his council. Next, Marco traveled southeast to the province of Manzi, which he described as the richest place in the world. In the city of Yangchow, Marco served as governor for three years.

A little to the south was the city of Kinsai, which means "city of heaven" in Chinese. Kinsai was one of the greatest centers of culture, education, and the arts the world has ever known. At that time there were more books in its library than in any other city on earth. With its canals, waterways, connecting bridges, and islands, Kinsai reminded Marco of Venice on a much grander scale. The great palace had twenty golden halls and a thousand rooms that dazzled the eye! He heard fantastic operas and extraordinary music on the pipa, chin, and horse-headed fiddle. He saw puppet shows, dances, and marvelous silk paintings everywhere!

Marco traveled to every province in China as the ambassador of Kublai Khan. His travels gained him a greater knowledge of the world than any other man who had ever lived before. Meanwhile, his father, Niccolo, and his uncle Maffeo had amassed great wealth by trading in gems. They were getting old, however, and wanted to return to Venice while they still had enough strength. Kublai Khan was getting old, too, and the Polos depended on his goodwill and protection. At court the Polos were greatly envied because of the Khan's favors, and if the emperor died, it was doubtful his successor would treat them as well.

Many times the Polos respectfully requested to leave, but the emperor depended on their loyal service and refused. Sixteen years passed, and the Polos were sure they would die in China. Then, in 1291, there came an opportunity for them to leave.

Arghun Khan, king of Persia and a great-nephew of Kublai Khan, had married a queen named Bolgana. In 1286 Queen Bolgana fell gravely ill. On her deathbed, she asked that her husband's next wife be a woman from her own Mongol clan. King Arghun Khan carried out her wish by sending three ambassadors to the court of Kublai Khan.

In 1288 the great Khan selected a beautiful seventeen-year-old princess named Cocachin to be Arghun's next queen. She was called "the blue princess" because her name means "blue like the sky." With great fanfare, the royal caravan departed overland for Persia. When the party came to the mountains of central Asia, it was attacked by rival Mongol warriors fighting for the territory, and so it returned to Khanbalik.

Marco Polo had just returned from a long voyage to India and Ceylon, where he had collected relics of the great buddha Shakyamuni for Kublai Khan's temple. At court the Persians listened to Marco's report of his seafaring journey and were highly impressed. They felt that Marco could safely take them back to Persia by ship. They put so much pressure on Kublai Khan that he finally consented.

The mighty Khan presented the Polos with two new gold tablets that would guarantee them safe passage and assistance throughout the Mongol empire. He also gave them diplomatic letters for the pope and kings of Europe as well as generous gifts of rubies and sapphires. Niccolo, Uncle Maffeo, and Marco Polo bade the emperor farewell and promised to carry out his mission.

At the Chinese port of Zaiton, the emperor Kublai Khan had ordered thirteen ships with ingenious water-tight compartments built for the Polos. The ships had been loaded with enough food and equipment to last two years.

In 1292 the Polos sailed on into the South China Sea. For 1,500 miles, they headed south to Champa, where Kublai Khan received his yearly tribute in elephants, incense, aloe, and ebony.

Farther south, they sailed past Java, which produced spices including black and white pepper.

Suddenly the monsoon storms began to blow, and the Polos were deluged by sweeping rains. They pitched their camp on the island of Sumatra for five months, all the while fearing native cannibals. There Marco discovered the sago palm, a tree filled with powdery starch that can be boiled into bread. For the first time he saw nuts "as big as a man's head," or coconuts. He described wild orange men with tails, or orangutans, and huge "unicorns nearly the size of elephants," or rhinoceroses!

When the weather cleared, the Polos sailed a thousand miles across the sea to Ceylon. They were amazed by the vast amounts of mined rubies, sapphires, topazes, and amethysts. In the gulf between India and Ceylon, Indian fleets carried hundreds of pearl fishermen who dived overboard to collect pearls that supplied the entire world market.

The royal fleet stopped at ports along the Indian Coramandel coast, where Marco said that "the heat was so great, you could boil an egg in an Indian river!" He described lions that were "black all over," or panthers. He described Hindus who worshipped the Brahma bull and believed in the reincarnation of souls—the idea that when you die, your soul is reborn again. Because of this idea, Hindus would not kill even a fly, flea, louse, or anything that has life, since all have souls. He also described Hindu yogis who wore hardly any clothes and their meditative practices.

In Guzerat, on the northwest coast of India, Marco was amazed by the enormously wealthy kings and princes draped in diamonds, pearls, rubies, sapphires, and gold who had thousands of servants and hundreds of wives. He also wrote of the Golconda diamond fields, which yielded the greatest stones in the world.

Leaving the northwest coast of India, Marco sailed into the Arabian Sea. He heard frightening stories of a terrible gigantic bird known as the roc that could seize an elephant in its beak and completely devour it.

Marco also had to watch out for gangs of Indian pirates traveling on as many as thirty ships. The pirates captured and robbed all the merchant ships in sight. Marco's fleet suffered accidents, storms, and sickness, and many of the crew died along the way. Out of the six hundred passengers that had left China, only eight survived, including Marco, Niccolo, Uncle Maffeo, and Princess Cocachin.

After two long years, Marco finally landed at the Persian seaport of Hormuz. But there the Polos learned that King Arghun Khan, to whom they were bringing Princess Cocachin, had died. It was soon decided that she would marry King Arghun's son and heir, Ghazan, and so the Polos celebrated the royal wedding and rested in Persia for nine months.

Finally, the Polos said a fond farewell to Queen Cocachin and, mounting their horses, headed north to the Persian city of Tabriz.

There they heard that the great Kublai Khan had died and realized they had made the right decision to leave China when they did. The Persian king presented the Polos with gold Persian passports and gave them a guard of two hundred horsemen to protect them on their journey ahead.

Day after day, they traveled north to Trebizond on the Black Sea. Unfortunately, in Trebizond the Polos were cheated out of some of the money and goods they had carried from China. But after twenty-four years of traveling, they began to hear news of their beloved city of Venice!

Boarding a ship, they sailed across the Black Sea to Istanbul. From there they entered the Mediterranean Sea. In the year 1295 they finally arrived back in Venice. For the first time in twenty-four years, they walked the streets of their homeland. There was San Marco Cathedral! There were gondolas! And there were ringing bells! Marco was then forty-one years old.

When the three Polos arrived home dressed in ragged sea clothes, none of their relatives recognized them. The family thought they had died long before. Only after sitting down together and sharing old family stories were the three Polos finally accepted. Still, no one believed the tales of golden pavilions, rubies, and rich treasure that were told by the three bedraggled men.

To prove they were telling the truth, the three Polos organized a great banquet paid for with some of the rubies, diamonds, emeralds, and sapphires they had sewn into the linings of their clothes.

Marco spoke of his adventures. He showed samples of sago-palm flour, seeds of Asian trees, and rubies from golden palaces. At first, many people were filled with wonder at his stories. Some thought Marco was boasting, some were bored, and some just laughed in his face!

At the time, Venice was at war with Genoa, and Marco wanted to help his city. He was appointed commander of a Venetian galley ship and steered bravely into battle. On September 7, 1298, the Battle of Curzola was fought in the Adriatic Sea. The Venetians lost, and Marco was captured. He was thrown into a crowded cell in Genoa's Palace San Giorgio and bound in chains.

To pass the time, Marco began to tell wonderful tales of his astonishing adventures. He spun stories of the holy oil from Jerusalem, assassins, marauding Mamluks and Mongols, and the fabled cities of Kublai Khan.

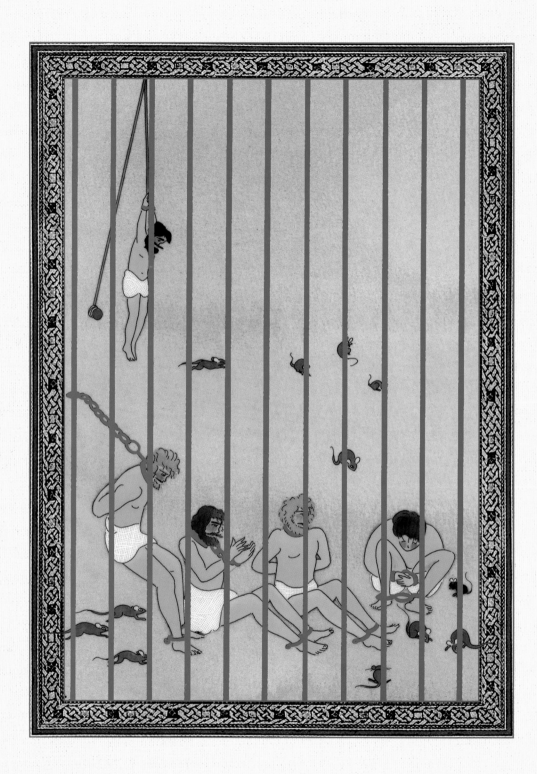

A prisoner from Pisa named Rustichello listened to Marco's tales. He was a skilled writer and understood how important Marco's stories would be to the world. He offered to write them down, and Marco happily agreed. Rustichello titled the book *Description of the World*, which later became *The Travels of Marco Polo*. Rustichello wrote, "There never was a single man before who learned so much and beheld so much." Marco wrote on the last page, "I believe it was God's pleasure that we should get back in order that people might learn about the things the world contains."

In the spring of 1299 the book was finished and a truce ended the war between Genoa and Venice. Marco returned home. He was forty-five, and he decided it was time to get married. He soon met Donata Badoer, and they married in San Lorenzo Cathedral. Shortly afterward they had three daughters: Fantina, Bellela, and Moreta.

From then on, Marco became a merchant of Venice. He organized trading ships and bartered for spices, gold, and jewels. But his life in Venice was dull compared to his wild adventures on the Silk Route to China and beyond. He told stories of his travel adventures a million times. He told of the millions of Chinese and the millions of gold pieces. Soon Marco was known as Marco Millions, and his house was called Millions Court.

Around 1300, Niccolo Polo died, and a few years later, so did Uncle Maffeo. Marco had lost two of the greatest explorers the world had ever known, and the two brilliant men who also knew the truth of his adventures.

From then on Marco was surrounded by ignorant people who only laughed at him. In 1323 Marco's health began to fail. On January 8, 1324, Marco dictated his final wishes and then passed away. He was buried in the Church of San Lorenzo beside the body of his father.

Marco left behind a wonderful treasure, *The Travels of Marco Polo*. This became a medieval best seller, and copies were translated by hand into all the European languages. His picture of such a vast wide world was more than most people could understand, and so his book was considered a wonderful fantasy. However, in time people began to see that Marco had been telling the truth all along. Merchants, mapmakers, historians, explorers, and religious scholars followed in his footsteps. Christopher Columbus used the *Travels* as one of his guides to the New World.

The Travels of Marco Polo is probably the greatest travel book ever written. Few people have lived fuller lives, faced more danger, or seen as much beauty and splendor as Marco Polo. The great merchant of Venice, ambassador, and fearless explorer lived and saw more than even he could tell.

It is said that while Marco Polo lay in bed at the end of his life, a priest—not wishing Marco to die with any lies on his conscience—asked him if he wished to take back some of the stories he had told. The wise explorer replied to the priest:

I did not tell half of what I saw,
for I knew I would not be believed!

GENOA

VENICE

RUSSIA

ITALY

Adriatic Sea

Mediterranean Sea

ISTANBUL
(CONSTANTINOPLE)

TURKEY

Black Sea

GEORGIA

TREBIZOND

ARMENIA
Mount Ararat
• TABRIZ

Caspian Sea

Aral Sea

Oxus River

BADAKSHAN

KASHGAR

PAMIR
MOUNTAINS

AYAS

ACRE
• JERUSALEM

BAGHDAD

PERSIA

TUNOCAIN

BALKH

HERAT

Nile River

Red Sea

ARABIA

Persian Gulf

KERMAN
*Rudbar
Plain*

Desert of Emptiness

(AFGHANISTAN)

Himalayas

TIBET

HORMUZ

INDIA

GUZERAT

AFRICA

*Arabian
Sea*

• THANA

INDIAN OCEAN

MONGOLIA

SIBERIA

Gobi Desert

SHANGTU
(XANADU)

CHAGON NOR • KHANBALIK
(Beijing)

SHACOW
(Dunghuang)

*East
China Sea*

LOP NOR

KANCHOW

Great Yellow River

SIAN • KAIFENG

*Taklimakan
Desert*

YANGCHOW

KOTAN

CHENGTU

CHINA

Yangtze River

KINSAI
(Hangchow)

MANZI
PROVINCE

ZAITON

**The Route
of
MARCO POLO**

BENGAL

—— MARCO'S ROUTE TO CHINA
—— MARCO'S RETURN HOME

BURMA

Mekong River

*South China
Sea*

Bay of Bengal

*Andaman
Island*

**CHAMPA
(VIETNAM)**

NICOBAR
ISLANDS

Maylay Penninsula

**CEYLON
(SRI LANKA)**

SUMATRA